PANDA

PANDA

written and illustrated by

CÉCILE CURTIS

大熊猫

FREDERICK WARNE

For Emma Curtis, with great affection

Published by Frederick Warne & Co Ltd
London, England
1976

ISBN 0 7232 1851 X

Printed in Great Britain by
Morrison & Gibb Ltd, London and Edinburgh
829.276

THE ARRIVAL

September 14th 1974 was the great day. Early that morning a large plane gleamed in the sun as it touched down at London's Heathrow airport after a twenty-hour flight with a very strange cargo. Most of the space inside was filled with great blocks of ice, masses of bamboo shoots and two over-sized oxygen masks, leaving just enough room for three Peking Zoo officials, three from the London Zoo, and the reason for it all in two enormous wooden crates with exotic Chinese writing on their sides.

These precious parcels were unloaded with the utmost care from the body of the aircraft on to a moving ramp. As they slowly descended dozens of news photographers strained forward trying frantically to catch the first glimpse of this wonderful gift from China to Britain—a pair of Giant Pandas. 'Chia-Chia' (which means in Chinese Most Excellent) the male, and 'Ching-Ching' (Crystal Bright) the female, faced opposite ends of their boxes so that the clicking cameras could see only one of the moon-round white faces with sad looking black eyes, peering through the bars. There was plenty of mischief in Ching-Ching, however, as she aimed a crafty swipe at a stray leaf of bamboo and the trouser leg of a nearby zoo-keeper!

The Pandas were soon driven off in a van travelling back eastward into London and Regent's Park Zoo where their special quarters and even greater excitement awaited them. Here were still more cameras as eager newsmen recklessly tried to climb over everything between themselves and the two unusual visitors from the orient. Chia-Chia and Ching-Ching of course were far too busy exploring their new home and tasting the fresh bamboo which had been grown in Cornwall especially for them, to bother much with the reporters or the crowds of excited onlookers that later pressed around the enclosure.

It was all very understandable when you realize that these are two of only seven Giant Pandas in the whole world outside of China, the other pairs being in Japan and the United States of America and a lone female in France. There are at present around fifty in Chinese zoos and perhaps no more than a few hundred left in the wild so they are, as well as being delightful, very rare creatures indeed.

A VERY SHORT HISTORY

Not much more than a century ago an adventurous Jesuit missionary from France, Père Armand David, was exploring a remote mountainous region of South-West China. In a farmhouse one day he saw a strange black-and-white skin of what appeared to him to be some kind of bear. He promptly set about the task of obtaining another one like it with the help of the local peasant community and soon afterwards was able to send an excellent pelt to a Paris museum, which was shortly followed by three more.

Although as an admirer of St Francis of Assisi the good priest did not approve the hunting or killing of animals, in this case he was so fascinated by the unusual markings of the skin that he was prepared to make an exception. So important did he believe this to be to the advancement of natural history that he even paid the hunters a large sum of money as a reward for getting the specimens and treating the furs to prepare them for their long journey back to Europe.

It was not known at the time that this was the coat of the Giant Panda which the Chinese called 'Beishung'. For five hundred thousand years the dense bamboo forests and cloud-covered heights of this virtually unknown area had hidden it from the rest of the world.

Sixty-seven years were now to pass before a live Giant Panda was taken, against tremendous odds, to the West in 1936 by an American woman, Ruth Harkness. Her small and helpless captive of barely two weeks old was called 'Su-Lin' and lived the rest of his short life—a mere eighteen months—in a zoo in Chicago, U.S.A.

Before this unique event hunters from many nations had shot or vainly attempted to capture a Panda alive and so the success of Ruth Harkness and her guides made scientific history as well as creating public interest in a new and almost unbelievable species.

It was not long, therefore, before other expeditions set out to bring back this rare and endearing creature. To date in fact just twenty-four Giant Pandas have appeared in zoos outside China. They are, and always have been, a major attraction wherever they appear and will remain a mystery for many years to come.

As we shall see . . .

HOME IN THE WILD

The habitat of our subject is most ideally suitable as a hiding place for mysteries. With its steep, snow-covered mountain ranges over 5000 metres high descending through forests of huge blossom-laden rhododendron trees to dense impassable bamboo jungles that drop down sharply to bottomless ravines, it is frightening to the bravest explorer. The whole scene is forever enshrouded with clouds, mist, snow and ice and hundred-year-old pines, their branches ghostly with hanging bear lichens adding to the strangeness of the hidden world. Spruce, silver fir and yews also mingle with the ever present bamboo, while down in the deep valleys during the short summer an assortment of wild flowers briefly bloom.

Everywhere the mountain torrents roar over glistening boulders to replenish the clear water of the numerous inland lakes.

The home of the Giant Panda lies mainly in the province of Szechwan in South-West China but extends a great deal further than was at one time believed. Some have been discovered on the high windy plateaus and hillsides of Eastern Tibet and as far afield as the Chinese provinces of Yunnan in the south and Shensi in the north-east. This vast area roughly forms a triangle of 800 kilometres in each direction, a probable area of 320,000 square kilometres. Some have even estimated the extent to be twice that size. Small wonder then that it is so difficult to count the number of Giant Pandas living there!

Male & female meet in a setting of Dragon Spruce (*Picea asperata*) and wild irises (*Iris kumenensis*)

Golden Takin (*Budorcas taxicolor bedfordi*)

The Chinese government has imposed laws against hunting and capture since 1949 and the World Wildlife Fund, whose purpose is the protection of wild creatures and the places where they live, uses, not surprisingly, a simplified drawing of the animal as its symbol.

The Giant Panda quite happily shares his great natural sanctuary with many other kinds of animals. Besides several types of deer, bear, leopard and lynx, there is also the rare golden takin, another mystery for zoologists. Here we find a strange mixture of goat and antelope with a ram-like face and horns similar to those of the musk ox. Despite his heavy clumsy body, about 250 kilos in weight, the takin is able to navigate the steepest cliffs with ease and would be the envy of any mountaineer.

Another golden companion in this luxuriant terrain is the shy, snub-nosed or snow monkey. Including its long tail it is almost $1\frac{1}{2}$ metres in length and the bright area of blue on its nose and brows gives the impression of a fancy dress mask. Leaping about, high in the trees upon the snow-ridged mountains, with its long mane of shining hair, it is a seldom seen but never forgotten sight.

Snow Monkey
(*Rhinopithecus roxellanae*)

Finally we must not forget that other panda who lives here too. The lesser, or red panda as he is sometimes called, does not really resemble his giant namesake at all, looking as he does more like a fox with his reddish fur and fine bushy tail—thereby giving rise to his nickname of fire fox. But we shall study this charming fellow in more detail later, focusing especially on his likeness or otherwise to his more famous cousin.

In spite of the size and ferocity of some of the animals who tread the same paths as the Giant Panda, there is little evidence that they ever attack him and he appears to live his solitary existence quite undisturbed in his beautiful, if forbidding, home in the wild.

A CLOSER LOOK

What is he really like, this creature so often described as a black and white bear? Certainly he has become familiar and much loved over the past forty-odd years. The rounded outlines and large head are very appealing with bold patterns of light and dark.

His total length, not including the stumpy 'tucked in' tail, is about 1.85 metres, so that standing up on his hind legs, which he is perfectly able to do, he is the height of a tall man. The bulky, massive body of an adult male reaches 140 kilos or more, the female weighing perhaps 25 kilos less. One of the things most noticeable on seeing a Panda for the first time is that the fur is not really just black and white but a great many other colours besides, ranging from yellow on the back and belly to grey and reddish brown particularly on the long tufts of hair at the outside of the wrists. Luckily the pelt has never been sought after by man for use as clothing or other purposes except perhaps occasionally in the past by a few peasants, as its coloration and coarseness have never been considered a great prize. Being long, thick and springy, it suits the Giant Panda very well, however, giving him an ideal protection against a cold damp climate. A further intriguing aspect of the fur is that it changes its direction of growth from between the eyes downwards to the tip of the large shiny black nose. The only other animals possessing this unusual feature are cats and bears.

Underside of right front paw showing the all-important 'thumb'
and (right) 'Chia-Chia' putting his to good use

Possibly the most interesting physical quality of the Panda is the curious 'thumb' on the forefoot. This appendage, used together with the first two claws, enables the animal to handle objects in an almost human way. One zoo inmate in China has been reported to feed herself soup with a spoon and it is quite commonplace to see Pandas lifting bowls of food to their mouths as a human baby will drink from a mug. The 'thumb' is used mostly for gripping the tough stems of bamboo, a principal item of diet, and even a small piece of bread will be handled with delicate skill. This digit is in fact a small bone covered with a thick pad. Smaller pads, like tiny pin-cushions, also exist at the base of each of the five claws and there are larger ones on the soles of all four feet. In between grow thick mats of rough hair which are not only a protection from sharp objects but also prevent slipping on ice and steep snow-covered ground.

The Giant Panda's first line of defence is unquestionably his powerful jaws and teeth set in a heavy skull. In fact the whole head seems to have been specifically designed for stripping and chewing tough bamboo stalks. He spends many of his waking hours engaged in doing just this, preferring then a sitting position which enables him to use both 'hands' at once.

If we were to see our black-and-white friend in silhouette with no markings to identify him, we should still know him quite readily by his outstanding way of walking. With head down and front feet turned awkwardly inwards, he travels in long slow strides, shoulders and hips rolling and head swaying from side to side.

The casual observer will have great difficulty in deciding from purely outward appearances the difference between male and female. Until quite recently, when more detailed studies became possible, many Pandas in zoos had lived for years being mistakenly sexed. There may be some slight variation in the texture of their fur, the female having perhaps a softer quality with smaller black areas. When they are fully grown, around the age of six, the male is usually heavier but even this is not always noticeable or reliable due to differences in individuals—just as with human beings. The male can be more inclined to bouts of temper and even aggression and is sometimes given to making a strange barking cry, whereas females are generally more sociable and playful. Both are fond of a frolic, especially when young, chasing each other and tumbling about with an affectionate nip now and then. But there are no hard and fast rules and only a precise physical examination can determine the gender of any animal.

This is yet another example of how little is really known about the Giant Panda and the mysteries that have long surrounded it and continue to exist.

THE QUESTION OF FAMILY

Of all the many unanswered questions concerning the Giant Panda, that of classification is one of the most puzzling.

Is he to be grouped with the bears, the raccoons or some other species, or is he a member of a family all his own? Experts on zoology have equally strong arguments in favour of one or another and we might well ask, 'Why does it matter?' First of all one could say that an exact understanding of an animal's nearest relatives helps scientists, zoo authorities and conservationists to know what to expect of various creatures both in captivity and in the wild, and gives some indication for their needs in a caged or natural environment. Secondly there is the problem of language. There are now well over 1,000,000 species of animals at present on earth known to science and the number grows every year. At first, in the days before natural history became an organized subject for study, those interested in wildlife would use their own particular language to name the creatures they wished to describe and this resulted in much confusion when studying reports from different lands. Then in 1757 a Swedish botanist who called himself Linnaeus introduced a system of names containing a mixture of Latin and Greek words only, and this method has been used ever since.

We already know that 'Beishung' means Giant Panda in Chinese but other names have been used at various times which described him as, 'Harlequin Bear', 'Bamboo Bear', and even a 'Bear-like Cat', this latter probably being due to an ability to climb, combined with a playful or cat-like disposition. After his initial discovery he

Himalayan Bear (*Selenarctos thibetanus*)

was, not without some reason, known in the western world as Père David's Bear.

Let us look at his full scientific title as it stands today. It is quite impressive and though it does not tell the full story we can learn quite a lot from it.

PHYLUM: Chordata (back-boned animal)
CLASS: Mammalia (bears live young which are suckled)
ORDER: Carnivora (meat-eater)
FAMILY: Procyonidae (raccoon)
GENUS: *Ailuropoda* (panda-footed)
SPECIES: *Melanoleuca* (black and white)

With some animals these terms are followed by the place the creature comes from or the name of the person who discovered it. Sometimes both.

The zoologist who firmly believes in the idea that the Giant Panda belongs to the bear family would not agree with the 'Procyonidae' or raccoon classification. Clearly the animal's size and form are more like the bear than anything else and indeed a near neighbour, the Himalayan black bear, even has a white crescent on the chest. There are however, noticeable differences in the teeth, shape of head and way of moving. For example, the bear is not only able to stand up on its hind legs but can easily walk in this manner as well, which the Panda cannot. Then there is the matter of the all-important 'thumb' which true bears do not possess and also they have no hair on the sole of the foot.

It is far more difficult to imagine that the Giant Panda belongs to the raccoon family—or at any rate to accept this belief—although it must be said that the lesser panda which is also in this group does seem to fit there more readily. It is much closer in size to the raccoon, being a mere 120 centimetres or so in length, tail included, and markings such as the dark rings on the long bushy tail and black and white on the short pointed muzzle are very much alike. Only in the colouring is there an obvious distinction. Although the raccoons also use their forefeet skilfully in a very 'handlike' way, they do not actually have the special 'thumb' and bamboo-eating habit of both Giant and lesser pandas. This in turn gives rise to yet another theory that these two belong in a separate family altogether that is strictly their own. Whilst the lesser panda's 'thumb' is not so developed, it is still a unique feature in both animals.

These arguments go on today with little likelihood that the question will be resolved in the near future. Only the Giant Panda himself seems unconcerned by it all and he is quite happy to let the experts worry whilst he gets on with the important job of just being one of the most fascinating animals on earth.

North American Raccoon (*Procyon lotor*)

Lesser Panda (*Ailurus fulgens styani*) feeding on
bamboo (*Phyllostachys aurea*)

WHAT HE EATS

As we know, the Giant Panda is classed as a meat-eater but in fact he only consumes small animals such as snakes, insects and a few birds on rare occasions when the bamboo is not at its best or is covered by too much snow. Then he must be very lucky to catch them as it would seem to be difficult with his slow clumsy movements. He is, nevertheless, surprisingly skilled at catching fish in the mountain streams which he does with one swipe of a broad flat forepaw.

Meat is not the only supplementary item of his diet in the wild. Pandas have sometimes been seen eating various vegetables, the bark of the Chinese fir, vines, rice grass, and even flowers such as irises and crocuses. They have also been known to raid bee hives in search of honey.

The animal is believed to have been more of a carnivore in prehistoric times but gradually the jaws and teeth grew more powerful and he adapted to a principally vegetarian diet.

It was once thought that bamboo was his only food. Certainly it is the main item in his diet which he manages to tuck away at the rate of 20 kilos a day—leaves, shoots, stems and all! It is not clear whether the Panda chooses the area that he inhabits because he is fond of the crisp, sweetish taste of bamboo or merely eats so much of it because it is plentiful.

When Giant Pandas began to be kept in zoos there was a great deal of concern about feeding them. The animals soon amazed their keepers by gobbling up just about everything they were offered, including such unlikely things as porridge, spaghetti and even jam! In addition all kinds of vegetables and fruit as well as rice, raw eggs and sugar were greedily accepted. In some cases they became much too fat of course and had to be put on a more balanced regimen—plenty of their local bamboo and only reasonable rations of the richer fare. One male in Moscow reached the remarkable weight of 185 kilos, probably because of a total lack of bamboo on his menu. Occasionally a small amount of roast chicken or beef is given to Pandas but they thrive mainly on two good meals a day, a healthful mixture of rice, maize, soya bean and bone meal plus sugar, salt and eggs. All the rest of the day of course they chew away at their favourite greenstuff.

It is likely that in the wild state the Panda seldom has much need to drink, living as he does in an atmosphere forever moist with rain and mist, but he seems to require water in captivity, drawing it up through the lips rather than lapping in cat fashion. Some have even shown a liking for condensed milk, drinking it straight from the tin with somewhat messy but no doubt well-enjoyed results!

Our plump friend is obviously a very adaptable fellow indeed and not at all the fussy eater he was once assumed to be.

'Ling-Ling' keeping her weight up at Washington Zoo

PERSONALITY AND BEHAVIOUR

The Giant Panda is usually described as a shy, timid creature, living his lonely life in a mountain wilderness which is his own special territory, except during the spring mating season when a pair will stay together for perhaps a month. But this is not strictly accurate for frequently a female will keep her infant with her for several years after birth—perhaps until the age of three or possibly more.

But solitary though many mature adults may be—especially the males—the creature has a lively and playful side to his nature, showing an interest in anything that can be used as a toy. This is reflected by his behaviour in captivity when such objects as swings, rubber tyres, ladders and feeding bowls provide endless hours of simple pleasure and amusement.

If somewhat clumsy and slow on the ground, the Panda more than makes up for his lethargy as a climber and aerial gymnast. He has been seen high in the branches of a tree neatly escaping hunters with dogs, or just reaching for the sun which seldom penetrates to the floor of the overgrown forest. In zoos he finds that high horizontal bars are excellent structures from which to swing. Somersaults and headstands are another favourite form of play.

When not occupied with the more serious business of munching at a tough branch, a good deal of time is devoted to sleeping, and he can put his head down virtually anywhere, even in the fork of a large tree. In his natural state he does build a sort of nest, however, though it is a fairly casual affair of leaves and broken twigs. These abandoned nests are seen in many places, under a dead tree-stump or overhanging rock, at the base or better still within, a hollow conifer. Caves too make good sleeping quarters but all are found to be quite a distance from feeding places and the animals do not use any particular one for very long, moving on from one to the other over a wide area. Pandas, unlike bears, do not hibernate in winter.

They tend to be sleepier in zoos where altitudes are very much lower than their natural home and there is not the need or opportunity to be so active.

As well as being an able climber, at least until he becomes very heavy, the Panda is quite capable of swimming and can even manage rushing mountain streams with ease. Zoo Pandas have been watched by delighted onlookers as they enjoy their baths, splashing around in tubs like young children. Being so accustomed to heavy rainfalls in their mountainous home it would seem only natural that they should find this a pleasant pastime.

As far as can be determined, the animal has poor eyesight but would appear to make up for it with excellent hearing, recognizing the voice of a particular person even after an absence of many months. A keen sense of smell is also useful in searching for the right kind of vegetation and judging its suitability as food.

Great care must be taken to see that they do not suffer from extreme heat in the summer as the highest temperature in their own habitat never rises above 20

degrees centigrade and in winter can drop to 7 degrees or more below zero. Many zoos provide air-conditioning during the hot months and large blocks of ice on particularly scorching days for their warm-coated guests. Their quarters are usually maintained at around 5 degrees in winter as extreme cold is not considered to be healthy for any length of time without the exertion they would normally experience in the wild.

Zoos always try to supply their charges with playthings to keep them amused and provide much needed exercise, a precaution not so necessary in the rare cases where there are two living together.

If an animal lives alone, as most zoo Pandas have in the past, then a keeper can be a good substitute as a playmate. This can sometimes unfortunately lead to tragic results as in the sad case of London's 'Chi-Chi'. For six years she had been a friendly amiable creature until one day, during what would have been her mating season in nature, she suddenly attacked and seriously injured one of her keepers for no apparent reason. After he had recovered, this young man naturally wanted to go back to look after her but she would have none of it.

This is just one of the mysteries about the Giant Panda whose behaviour at times can be as perplexing as it is amusing.

A GIANT PANDA IS BORN

It is late October. Down through the evergreen and bamboo forests silent with winter, a solitary female Panda descends with difficulty through the deepening snow.

On the lower slopes she will find shelter from the sharp winds and the undergrowth will not be so laden down with the white blanket that covers it high above.

Five months earlier she and her husky male companion had chased each other along green mossy banks and through dappled sunshine that found and highlighted patches of brilliant blooms. Their loud bleating cries echoed in the dense woods and out across the rocky ravines.

Now her breath forms a mist in the cold air and in her slow journey downward the heavy figure stops many times, here to inspect an old tree stump, there to briefly enter a small cave whose entrance is partially hidden by fresh snow, then over to a deep depression at the base of an overhanging rock. Further on, within the range of her short-sighted vision, stands an ancient hollow tree—a half-forgotten sleeping place. She sniffs it carefully, shifting remains of rotting leaves and fibrous stalks. Soon she begins to busy herself collecting fresh vegetation, selecting it carefully until, satisfied at last, she can crawl deep inside and settle down for the approaching night.

As the next days pass, most of the time is spent eating and sleeping in the comfort of the old tree with its shelter from the bitter winds and driving snow, and she will only leave this haven for short periods to a nearby thicket to replenish her supply of food.

Then, early one morning the baby is born. It scarcely seems possible that this tiny bundle, about the size of a small kitten and weighing a mere 100 grammes, can really be the offspring of the huge magnificent animal who holds it so tenderly in her broad forepaws.

The mother will now sit for several days gently rocking and will neither eat nor sleep, her blind, helpless newly-born with its sparse covering of white hair almost hidden against the long fur of her warm body.

For several weeks she will continue to cradle the baby in her arms even while she is eating, and to soothe it with tender caresses when she feels it is in need of comfort, in much the same manner as a human mother.

When the brownish-black coat thickens under the white guard hairs and the grey-brown fur forms a soft warm covering over its belly, the mother will begin to play with the young Panda, throwing it from one arm to the other and even holding it upside down at times which seems to amuse them both!

Three months will pass before the cub is able to leave the warmth of its mother's arms for the first time and stagger forth on initial unsteady steps. It is not yet to be allowed to wander very far and is soon brought back with a gentle sweep of a protective paw. As growing up proceeds, the mother indulges in more active play, rolling about with her young one like a youngster herself, and it is difficult to say which of them frolics with the most delight. She is still very protective and will climb trees with her child clinging to her back.

After six months when the young Panda is weaned it will weigh about 10 or 12 kilos and will be more capable of looking after itself. With the warmer weather approaching there will be tender grasses, plants and flowers, as well as the young bamboo shoots to eat, but it will be another six months before the permanent teeth arrive and the tougher stalks can be chewed.

Nearly two years must pass before the mother once again seeks shelter for the birth of another Panda infant.

PANDAS AROUND THE WORLD

Most of the Giant Pandas in past and present captivity in the West have been world famous and it is not possible to tell all their histories here. Two of the best known in recent years were 'Chi-Chi' and 'An-An'. In 1966 great efforts were made by both the London and Moscow zoos to mate these two animals. Regent's Park had been the home of the female, 'Chi-Chi', for eight years since her arrival as a bouncy, healthy one-year-old who soon lived up to her name which means 'Naughty Little Girl' by climbing a fence and running into the crowd on two occasions. Moscow's 'An-An' was about the same age and had spent an equal period in the Russian zoo in solitary splendour. The two institutions decided that the time was right to

Mother with two-week old infant sheltering in a
hollow pine (*Pinus wallichiana*)

attempt breeding.

'Chi-Chi' left London for her six-month visit to the prospective husband amid much publicity and high hopes by the authorities that there would be a successful outcome. It was all in vain. She refused, despite repeated meetings, to be at all friendly with him and much preferred the company of her keepers. When 'An-An' was flown over to visit her in London for another six-month trial two years later, the result was the same. The sad conclusion was that a Panda who has spent so many years without ever seeing another of its own kind is very unlikely to be capable of mating. A number of recent studies of animals in captivity, shows that, if solitary, they do not recognize their own kind but actually believe themselves to be human beings.

Both 'Chi-Chi' and 'An-An' lived their separate lives until the age of fifteen (dying within a few months of each other), the longest time thus far for zoo Pandas, although the animal is said to survive for twenty-five to thirty years in the wild state.

There have been other stories with happier endings. Perhaps the greatest celebrities of all are the female 'Li-Li' from the great modern zoo at Peking together with her cub 'Ming-Ming'. 'Li-Li means Beautiful and 'Ming-Ming' means Brilliant. The double form of the names in Chinese is a term of endearment as we might precede a child's name with 'dear little . . .' but it is also a means of emphasizing a word so that it could be said that 'Li-Li' for example is a *Very* Beautiful *Dear Little* Giant Panda!

Of course 'Ming-Ming' is now no longer a cub as he was born in September 1963. This

'Ming-Ming' at about three months

is a very important event in zoo history and he will always be known as a very special baby, being the first Panda ever bred in captivity.

Normally a mother produces young every other year but it was no more than a year afterwards when 'Li-Li' presented her delighted hosts with yet another cub, the female 'Lin-Lin' or Pretty Jade. She was one of twins though the other cub did not survive. It was an outstanding occurrence for the Peking zoo and the whole world.

The Chinese Government have now given a number of other countries not only the priceless gift of Panda pairs but hope that they may in turn produce offspring as well.

CHIA-CHIA AND CHING-CHING AT HOME IN LONDON

Ever since the red banners flew at the London Zoo saying, in Chinese as well as English, 'Welcome to the two Giant Pandas from China' Chia-Chia and Ching-Ching have been welcome guests indeed, with many thousands of visitors. Their daily displays of circus-like performances are almost non-stop shows.

Chia-Chia was about twenty-two months old and weighed 49 kilos when he arrived and Ching-Ching was only a kilo heavier and a month older than her playmate. They were both captured at the age of six months in the Chinese province of Szechwan. She was found in the northern area near the Wanglang Nature Reserve and he came from many miles away in the eastern part of the territory. These two events were no mean accomplishment on the part of the resourceful Chinese naturalists, for as we know, it is a very difficult terrain to cover and one may well travel for many days before ever seeing a single Panda.

The pair lived together for a year in Peking zoo before their historic journey westward to the British Isles and have been quite rightly described by their Chinese hosts as 'very compatible'. They are certainly active and playful with their own particular brand of mischief, giving back as good as they get with almost tireless enthusiasm.

Let us pay them a visit at the London Zoo . . .

Their present enclosure is equipped with thick wooden pillars, tubs of water and bamboo plants. A rustic ladder has been thoughtfully placed against a stout tree, or at least the main lower part of one. Overhead is the complicated network of a climbing frame in which the plump performers make their way with amazing daintiness like the most expert of tightrope walkers. Besides a bathtub there are hollows filled with sawdust and silver sand which serve as a method of 'dry-cleaning', though to look at the Pandas' tough thick coats one wonders quite how this works. The 'white' fur is more of a pale, honey-brown, and the black areas are often speckled with bits of sawdust, giving them a rough and tumble appearance which is nonetheless very endearing, though at these times Ching-Ching's name which, as we remember, means 'Crystal Bright' does not seem very apt.

In the middle of everything hangs the Pandas' first Christmas present a huge lorry tyre suspended on a chain, which was described as 'just what they wanted'. It had been greeted initially with skittish suspicion but soon became a favourite toy and has proved to be suitably panda-proof.

We are warned that these animals are active in the morning and afternoon and usually sleep during the middle of the day, but this is not always so, especially on a damp cold day which is their favourite kind of weather when they are apt to have a romp at any time.

The two are lolling about on a strong wide branch of their tree and soon a boxing contest commences with a good deal of biting besides. When the nip is too fierce, a yelp of protest follows and the game quickly turns into a wrestling match, the object being to knock the opponent down to the ground. Chia-Chia finally forces Ching-Ching backwards down the ladder, her round bottom bumping against the rungs.

We can tell which Panda is which only when Ching-Ching turns her back to us and we can see that the band of black across her shoulders is much narrower than the male's. In fact it seems to almost disappear at the centre in a thin line. At times we can also notice that Chia-Chia is slightly bigger.

After a hasty somersault, the fallen female makes a dash over to the sawdust where she has a quick tumble. Chia-Chia hurries down the ladder and heads straight for the water tub. Resting his front paws on the edge, he enjoys a long thirsty drink as well he might after his many mouthfuls of dusty fur during the friendly battle. He then carefully dips his back feet into the water, one at a time and for reasons known only to himself.

This wooden tub is a great source of childish squabbles. One Panda only needs to see the other enjoying a bath and immediately wants to get in as well, untroubled

by the fact that there is barely enough room for one, let alone two. After much nudging and splashing the first bather good-naturedly moves out, appearing to leave rather more water outside the tub than in.

After his drink, Chia-Chia trots over to the bamboo where he tucks in noisily, munching the stalks held in both hands in an obvious effort to keep his strength up.

Now the tyre attracts him and he rolls on to his back underneath it, clutching it with all four paws. There is no room for Ching-Ching to join in the fun so she clutches him instead, biting the nape of his neck sharply just for good measure.

Tiring of this, she rushes back to the tree, eager to have it to herself, and after another swift somersault at the base, we can hear the sound of her sharp claws as she begins to climb. She works her way craftily to a place on the metal frame right over Chia-Chia and, dangling upside down with only her stubby back legs supporting her, makes several swipes at him, vainly trying to reach his head. He promptly scrambles up one of the group of tall pillars below her and tries to reach her with two legs spread awkwardly spanning two pillars and a front paw on a third. Finally, after trial and error, he succeeds in standing up straight enough to clasp Ching-Ching's shoulders and gives her a few smart bites around the face. With one more great effort he pulls himself on to the rail beside her, and then starts a perilous chase along the network of bars followed by another boxing and biting session on the tree branch. Chia-Chia shields one eye from the blows with her paw and the two tumble down the ladder to the ground, the female ending with a flourish in yet another of her swift somersaults.

The fascinated audience applauds loudly after this splendid show. In a few moments the two Pandas are back in the tree again, one with head resting on the other's back, front paws clasping it tightly and both are soon fast asleep.

Ching-Ching gained about 24 kilos in the first year at the London Zoo while Chia-Chia increased his weight twice as much as she, reaching a solid 97 kilos as a result of carefully planned meals. Twice a day, away from the eyes of an eager public they are fed separately on specially prepared dishes of meal mixed with an egg to which is added rather lumpy-looking rice. Over it all a pint of milk is poured and this food is served quite warm so that the animals will be tempted by its appetizing smell. As with many orientals, rice is an important part of their diet and is now believed to be especially so during a Panda's breeding season. When this time arrives, the male and female tend to replace their energetic games with fierce fighting at the beginning and have to be separated for a while until the female is actually ready to mate. The Chinese have taught us much in recent years with their valuable experience in successful breeding. Great care will be taken with Chia-Chia and Ching-Ching to see that they do not become too tame and familiar with humans. The keepers handle them as little as possible so that the failure of Chi-Chi and An-An to produce offspring will not be repeated.

The London pair will one day move into larger quarters where there is to be even more space for them and, if all goes according to plan, there will be room for a third . . .

'Ching-Ching' and 'Chia-Chia' after a hard day's play

HSING-HSING AND LING-LING AT HOME IN WASHINGTON

In April 1972 the United States received a pair of young Pandas as a gift from the Government of China. For many years the country had not possessed a single specimen, the last, 'Mei-Lan' having died at the age of fourteen in Chicago in 1953.

The very long journey from China to America was something of a problem but this was cleverly solved by the Chinese zoo authorities who arranged for the two animals to be taken for a trial flight to accustom them to air travel. During the trip to the States the Pandas were accompanied by various Peking zoo officials and keepers who not only nursed them carefully through the flight but remained nearby for some time while they settled in their new home. Interestingly, there was a stopover at Guam in the Pacific where fresh supplies of bamboo, especially collected in advance, were taken on board, and again at Hawaii where a similar meal-break had been organized. Finally, to the intense relief of all concerned, the two young animals stepped hesitantly out of the handsome green-lacquered boxes

'Hsing-Hsing'

in fine condition to inspect and obviously approve of the air-conditioned apartments.

There could not have been a warmer and more joyful welcome than that which awaited the two Pandas at this moment.

'Hsing-Hsing' (pronounced Shing-Shing) the male, was a year old on his arrival at the National Zoological Park in Washington D.C. and weighed approximately 34 kilos, while his female partner 'Ling-Ling' who is six months older weighed a chubby 61 kilos. She is heavier for her age because of her longer time in a zoo, but the male will eventually catch up and it is likely that he will in fact outweigh her when they are both fully grown.

'Hsing-Hsing' was a bit shy at first but his mate needed no encouragement to show off and play the clown, delighting her audience by wearing her feeding dish like a hat just when cameras were about to click!

Amongst the many efforts to keep the new arrivals happy was the search for suitable toys for the playful youngsters. It was not so easy as might have been supposed. Sturdy rubber basket-balls seemed a good choice but in the event 'Ling-Ling' chewed hers to ribbons within a few hours and 'Hsing-Hsing's' lasted barely a day longer. Next, some ordinary footballs were tried but these suffered the same fate. Only metal beer kegs survived the test until some specially designed plastic-covered balls proved to be hardy enough for sharp claws and powerful teeth. Both Pandas were so pleased with their new playthings that they ended up by hugging

'Ling-Ling'

them. They also liked big, multi-coloured plastic rings which they would wear like lifebelts and roll about in.

The two will live separately in their own individual apartments complete with air-conditioned indoor quarters and sleeping dens until they are fully matured. They can see each other through the wire-meshed fence in the outdoor play areas where they enjoy quick plunges in the rosewood bath tubs on hot summer days.

As they browse and sport in these tree-shaded enclosures, planted with bamboo and sweet-tasting tufted grasses, it is to be hoped that they will continue a contented and healthy life and perhaps soon there will be a cause for celebration, a baby Panda to keep them company.

THE FUTURE OF THE PRECIOUS FEW

Now for perhaps the first time the future for the Giant Panda seems to be brightening. The diligent Chinese have, over the past thirty years, made really admirable efforts to protect them from collectors and hunters who are tempted by their enormous value. The people of China have been taught to treat the animal as a National Treasure which indeed it is. A number of nature reserves have now been established, including one at Wanglang in Szechwan which covers an area of about 200 square kilometres. For the first time scientists can now observe and photograph the magnificent and little known habitat of this equally awe-inspiring creature.

Zoos in other parts of the world are gaining by the experience of Chinese zoologists in the care of these and other rare animals. In turn, the U.S.A. has presented China with a pair of rare North American musk oxen. In 1957 Britain gave four Père David's deer, animals which originally came from China, and another four at the same time that Chia-Chia and Ching-Ching were sent to London.

These deer have a curious as well as interesting history. The first westerner to observe them was the same keen naturalist and missionary who found the Giant Panda, but it is the deer rather than the Panda which is most often associated with him and still bears his name. He first saw them in the Imperial Hunting Park in Peking in 1865. His description was of a beast with stag's antlers, cow's hooves, a camel's neck and the tail of a donkey. It is not surprising that he was immensely pleased to be allowed to ship several of these unusual creatures to European zoos. It was indeed a fortunate twist of fate as the animal shortly afterwards became extinct in its native land. Now, after all those years, the Chinese hope to re-establish it in the country of its origin from stock which was bred abroad.

The Giant Panda, though not extinct, is without doubt very rare even by the most optimistic estimates. Perhaps it might not be too improbable to think that one day Pandas bred abroad might be sufficiently numerous to return some of them to their natural habitat as well. But of course this happy possibility is likely to be a long way off.

We have studied this appealing subject from many different vantage points. Much has been said about the little that is known thus far and a good deal about that which is not. The mysteries that surround him still persist. The glowing terms one can use by way of description are rich and plentiful. Amiable, acrobatic and adorable, bouncy, bearlike and beautiful, clownish, cuddly, cheeky and coy, one could go right through the alphabet. Certainly his charm is totally irresistible and Pandas will always be a star attraction wherever they appear.

Perhaps we should just remind ourselves that these enchanting creatures, despite their toy-like familiar appearance, are really wild animals, as wild and strange as the remote world from whence they come.

If you are fortunate in visiting a zoo where one or a pair can be seen then study them long and well. They are the precious few.

ACKNOWLEDGEMENTS

The author would like to express appreciation to the following for their kind assistance in the preparation of this book:

Tony Dale, Press Officer, Zoological Society of London; Liu Yü-Hua, Director, Peking Zoological Garden; Charles Jeffrey, B.A. (Camb), Principal Scientific Officer, and George Brown, Assistant Curator of the Arboretum, Royal Botanic Gardens, Kew; Kenneth Milsom, A.L.A. (on this occasion and so many others), Librarian in Charge, Wimbledon Library; Betty Patterson, Librarian, Society for Anglo-Chinese Understanding.

Also, special thanks to George Horton, B.Sc. (Lond) who went to endless trouble; Miriam Kahal Hughes, who kept me so well informed from her side of the Atlantic; and finally but so importantly, Master Mark Taylor, for his interest and criticism.